Contents

The children's hospital

A children's hospital is a place where children go to get better if they are ill or injured. They go in for tests or to see a doctor or nurse.

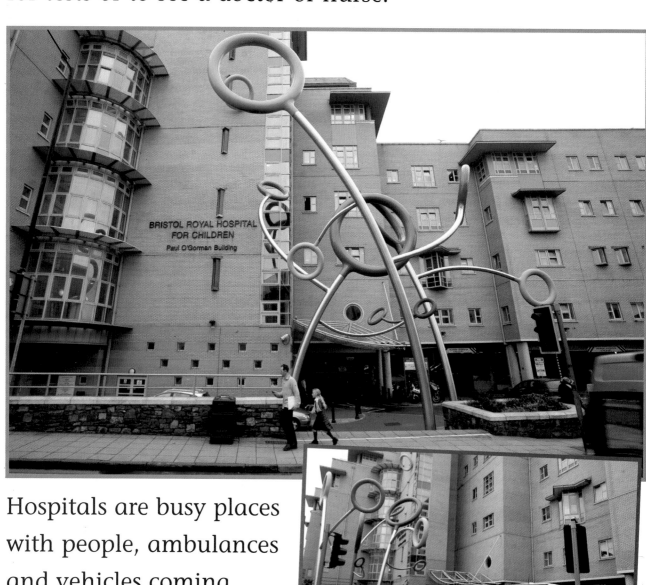

Hospitals are busy places with people, ambulances and vehicles coming and going.

In this hospital, there is a big **reception** area where people can get information.

There are lots of **wards** in the hospital. A ward is where **patients** stay so that doctors and nurses can **examine** and treat them.

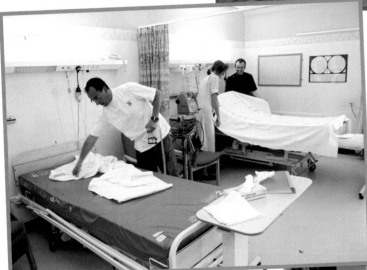

There are also **departments** that do special tests or certain **treatments**. All the test results are stored in an office.

The teams

Each ward has a team of doctors, nurses and other staff. The teams work together to make sure patients get the care and treatment they need.

Sarah is a nurse. One of her jobs is to take **samples** of blood to be used for **blood tests**.

Amy works in the **physiotherapy** department. She helps patients get better by helping them to do **exercises**.

June is part of a team that works to keep the hospital clean.

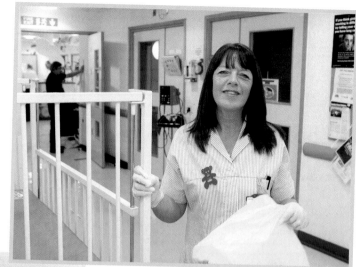

Sam is a play **specialist**. Her job is to keep patients happy. She works with patients in a playroom or visits them on the wards.

Aston is a **porter**. He works all over the hospital. Aston moves beds to where they are needed, as well as delivering post and taking out rubbish.

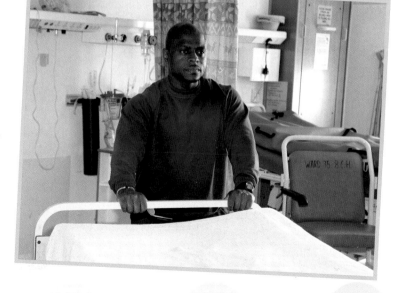

Starting work

In the reception area, Barbara is ready to greet visitors.

In a ward playroom, Sam sets up a table of toys for the patients.

Physiotherapist Amy chats with Janey, a nurse. They look at a list of patients to see who Amy needs to work with.

Sue works in a department that does tests on patients' hearts. She checks her computer to find out who she is going to see today.

Chris is a nurse. He checks his **emails** in the office before he starts work on one of the wards.

In the schoolroom

There is a schoolroom in the hospital. Teachers make sure that patients keep up with their schoolwork while they are staying in the hospital.

Here, teacher Jo starts her day by helping Lauren with some sums.

As patients and visitors arrive in reception, Barbara gives them all the help they need.

All the hospital post is dropped off at the reception. Barbara sorts the post for all the different parts of the hospital.

Porter Phil puts the post in a trolley. Then he delivers it to all the wards, offices and departments.

There are seats in the reception, where patients can wait to be collected to go home.

'It's a big, busy building, so people often need help to find their way around.'
Barbara, receptionist

Helping patients

Lisa works in an office in the reception. She works for PALS, a team that helps patients and their families.

PALS
Patient Advice
&
Liaison Service

Lisa gives people advice and information about coming into the hospital.

Going into hospital

Terrianne has come into hospital to have tests and to be seen by a doctor. First, nurse Chris talks to Terrianne's mum about the tests Terrianne needs.

Then Chris takes Terrianne's temperature with a **thermometer** that goes in her ear.

Doctor Fauzia checks Terrianne's ears for any problems.

Terrianne is upset by the different tests. She does not understand that the doctors and nurses are trying to help her.

Play specialist Sam keeps Terrianne happy while she has a blood sample taken.

Sam plays with Terrianne while she waits to see another doctor.

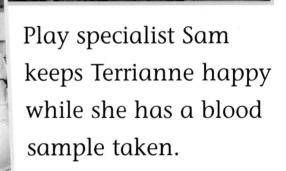

Looking after patients

Chris works on the wards, looking after patients and helping to treat them.

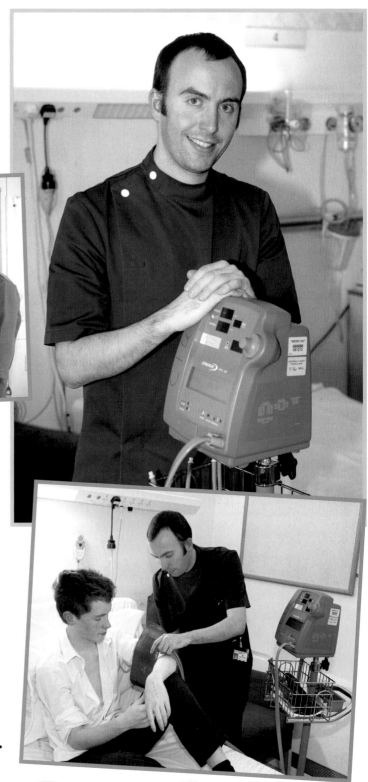

Doctor Fauzia talks to Chris about a new patient, William. She asks Chris to do a **blood pressure** test.

Chris takes William's blood pressure, and lets Fauzia know the **results**.

Chris also has to check the medicine supplies in the storeroom.

'We work closely with the doctors and other staff to make sure each patient gets the best care.'
Chris, nurse

Keeping in touch

Staff who work all over the hospital carry a bleep like this one. If a nurse needs a doctor or a porter to come to the ward, they can bleep this machine. A number comes up and shows who is trying to contact them.

Examining patients

Lisa is a doctor. She spends most of her day examining and treating patients. Here, she checks William's eyes.

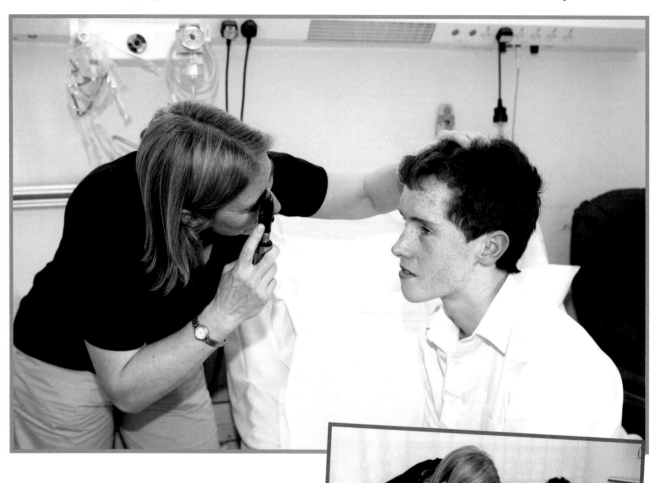

Lisa writes a **prescription** for William. This is a list of any **medicines** he needs.

'Finding the right treatment to help patients get better is very rewarding.'
Lisa, doctor

Lisa talks to Fauzia about more treatment for William. Then Lisa writes about the treatment in the patient notes.

Taking an x-ray

Here, Tom is having an **x-ray** of his arm. This shows how it is injured or why it hurts.

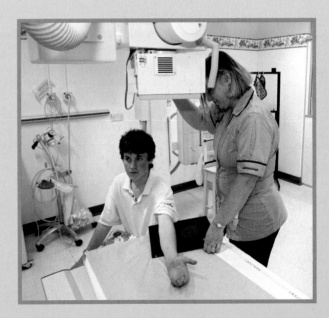

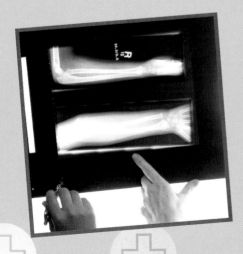

The doctor looks at the x-ray to help decide on the right treatment.

Heart tests

Lisa is listening to William's heart with a **stethoscope**.

If Lisa can hear a problem with a patient's heart she asks for more tests to be done.

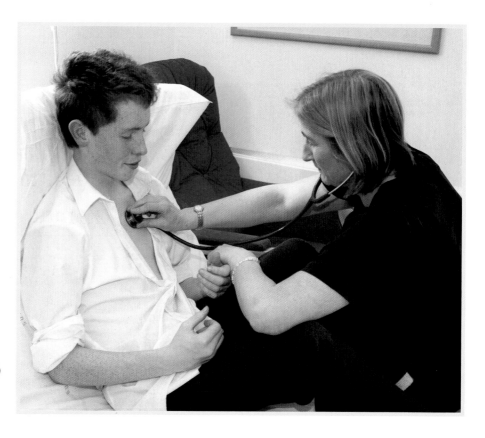

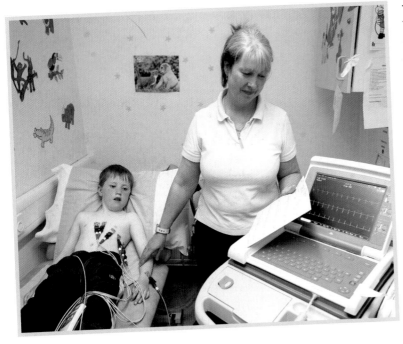

Mandy works in the heart department. She does a test that shows how Ollie's heart is beating. The machine prints out information about Ollie's heart.

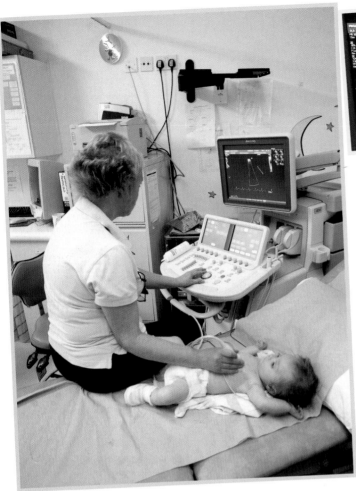

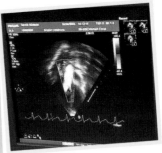

Sue does a different heart test. This machine picks up information about baby Roman's heart.

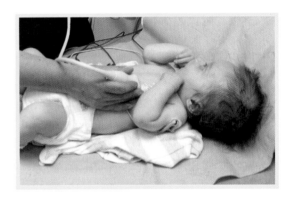

Test results

All the test results are put in the patient notes. These tests give the doctors information to help them decide on the best treatment.

In the operating theatre

The operating theatre is a place where patients have **operations**.

Doctors who do the operations are called **surgeons**.

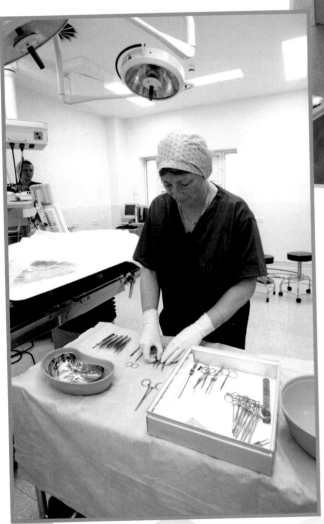

Michael is a surgeon. He is washing his hands before an operation.

Nurse Maria sets out all the **instruments** the surgeon might need for the operation.

Victoria and Peter get patients ready for operations by giving them medicine so they sleep and do not feel anything.

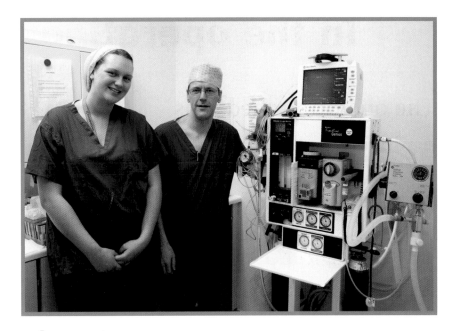

This operation is to take out the patient's **tonsils**.

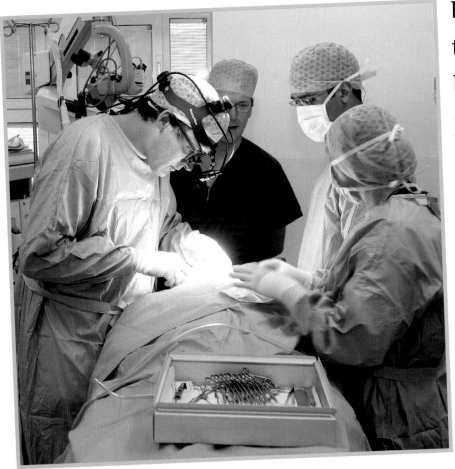

Blue cloths cover the patient's body so only the part the surgeon is working on shows. Michael wears a torch on his head so he can see clearly.

 Physiotherapy

Physiotherapy is using exercises to help patients get better.

Amy goes to the office to check her notes on the best exercises to use for one of her patients.

Amy helps Megan do some exercises in the gym. Megan needs help to walk after a hip operation.

Amy also goes to the wards to work with patients. Amy helps Lauren do some exercises to help her breathing.

Amy works in the pool with Oliver. He is doing exercises to help his sore knee that will not bend.

Food and drinks

Jackie is a cook. She works in the kitchen making meals for patients, visitors and for hospital staff.

In the reception, there is a board to show the canteen menu for the day.

Rachel and Mariama work in the kitchen. They cut up vegetables ready to be cooked

Jackie takes the baked potatoes out of the oven.

Jackie puts out drinks, salads and sandwiches in the canteen.

Nurse Chris takes a break from the ward to buy his lunch in the canteen.

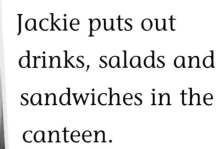

Housekeeping and cleaning

Pauline is a housekeeper. She helps to make sure the wards are clean and tidy and check that the patients have all that they need.

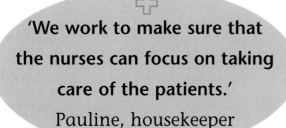

'We work to make sure that the nurses can focus on taking care of the patients.'

Pauline, housekeeper

Pauline checks the linen cupboard and makes sure there are enough clean sheets and blankets to go on the beds.

June works hard to keep her ward clean and tidy. She washes and polishes the floors.

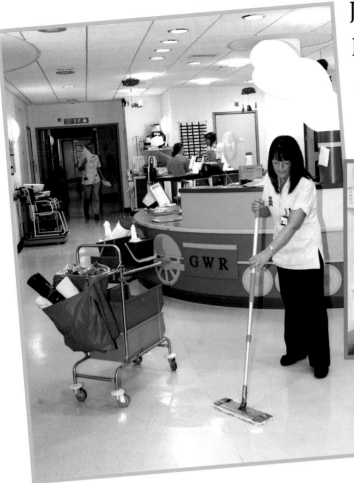

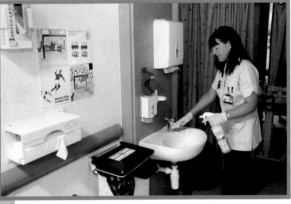

She cleans all the sinks and other equipment.

Killing germs

Each ward has a bottle of special gel by the door. People squirt the gel on their hands and rub it in. This helps to stop people spreading or catching **germs**.

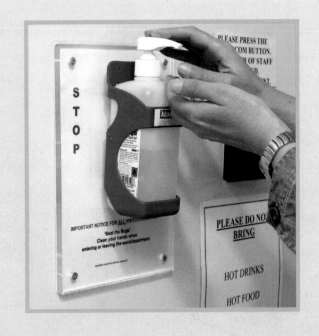

⊕ Finishing work

At the end of the day Amy writes up her physiotherapy patients's notes.

Pauline takes a prescription down to the **pharmacy** as her last job of the day. She also collects some medicines for a patient.

Sue types up the tests she has done before she finishes work.

Porter Aston moves one of the huge bins of hospital waste out to be emptied.

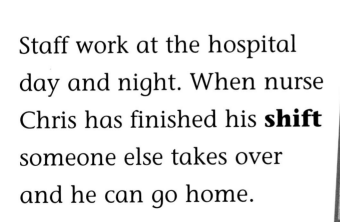

Staff work at the hospital day and night. When nurse Chris has finished his **shift** someone else takes over and he can go home.

Glossary

blood pressure a measurement of how fast blood is being pumped around the body by the heart.

blood test looking at a sample of blood to find out about how a body is working.

department part of a place, such as a hospital, specialising in one thing.

email messages sent by computer.

examine to look at carefully.

exercises movements of the body to make it better or fitter.

germs tiny living things that can cause illness or infection.

instruments tools used by a surgeon or doctor.

medicine something a doctor gives to help illness or pain.

operation repairing or removing something in the body.

patients people who are ill or injured, and who are being treated by a doctor.

pharmacy a place where medicines are prepared and handed out.

physiotherapy using exercises and massage to treat people who are injured.

porter a person who works carrying or moving things.

prescription written notes from a doctor giving details of a medicine to be given to a patient.

reception a place in a building to welcome visitors.

results numbers or diagrams to show what a test has found out.

samples small amounts of liquid or material.

shift period of time worked by people.

specialist a person who does one thing very well.

stethoscope an instrument used to listen to sounds in the body.

surgeon a doctor who repairs injured parts of a patient's body.

thermometer an instrument to measure how hot something is.

tonsils two small round lumps at the back of the mouth.

treatment medicines or surgery to make a patient better.

ward a room with lots of beds in a hospital.

x-ray a picture that shows bones and other parts inside the body.

Further information

Websites

www.ubht.nhs.uk/bch/ Visit this site to find out more about the Bristol Royal Hospital for Children.

www.bhf.org.uk/cbhf/ The British Heart foundation site for children, with facts and activities about how to keep your heart healthy.

www.childrenfirst.nhs.uk/ An interactive guide to health and hospitals.

Books

Your Body (Look After Yourself series), Claire Lewellyn, Franklin Watts, 2002.

At the Hospital (People Who Help Us series), Deborah Chancellor, Franklin Watts, 2003.

Every effort has been made by the Packagers and Publishers to ensure that these websites contain no inappropriate or offensive material. However, because of the nature of the Internet, it is impossible to guarantee that the contents of these sites will not be altered. We strongly advise that Internet access is supervised by a responsible adult.

Index